A Day in the Life: Rainforest Animals

Lemur

Anita Ganeri

www.raintreepublishers.co.uk
Visit our website to find out more information about Raintree books.

To order:
Phone 0845 6044371
Fax +44 (0) 1865 312263
Email myorders@raintreepublishers.co.uk

Customers from outside the UK please telephone +44 1865 312262

Raintree is an imprint of Capstone Global Library Limited, a company incorporated in England and Wales having its registered office at 7 Pilgrim Street, London, EC4V 6LB – Registered company number: 6695582

First published in hardback in 2011

Edited by Nancy Dickmann, Rebecca Rissman, and Catherine Veitch
Designed by Steve Mead
Picture research by Mica Brancic
Originated by Capstone Global Library
Printed and bound in China by South China Printing Company Ltd

ISBN 978 1 4062 1783 4 (hardback)
14 13 12 11 10
10 9 8 7 6 5 4 3 2 1

British Library Cataloguing in Publication Data
Ganeri, Anita
Lemur. -- (A day in the life. Rainforest animals)
599.8'3-dc22
A full catalogue record for this book is available from the British Library.

Acknowledgements
We would like to thank the following for permission to reproduce photographs: Alamy **pp. 10** (© Martin Harvey), **20** (© Fotosonline/Peter Kelly); Ardea **pp. 6** (M. Watson), **16** (Thomas Marent); Corbis **p. 12** (Encyclopedia/© Gallo Images); FLPA **pp. 4**, **19**, **23 mammal** (David Hosking), **15**, **23 fossa** (Ariadne Van Zandbergen), **17** (Jurgen & Christine Sohns), **21** (Albert Visage), **22** (Minden Pictures/ Thomas Marent); Photolibrary **pp. 5** (John Warburton-Lee Photography/Nigel Pavitt), **7**, **9**, **13**, **23 tuft** (Tips Italia/John Devries), **11** (Picture Press/ Jurgen & Christine Sohns), **18** (Oxford Scientific (OSF)/David Haring/DUPC); Photoshot **pp. 14**, **23 troop** (NHPA/Kevin Schafer); Shutterstock **p. 23 rainforest** (© Szefei).

Cover photograph of a black and white ruffed lemur hanging upside down in a tree reproduced with permission of Getty Images (Gallo Images/Martin Harvey).

Back cover photographs of (left) fossa reproduced with permission of FLPA (Ariadne Van Zandbergen); and (right) young lemur reproduced with permission of FLPA (David Hosking).

We would like to thank Michael Bright for his invaluable help in the preparation of this book.

BB
DCPL0000434191

YR

Contents

What is a lemur? 4
What do lemurs look like? 6
Where do lemurs live? 8
What do lemurs do in the day? 10
What do lemurs eat? 12
Do lemurs live in groups? 14
What do lemurs sound like? 16
Where are baby lemurs born? 18
What do lemurs do at night? 20
Lemur body map 22
Glossary 23
Find out more 24
Index 24

Some words are in bold, **like this**. You can find them in the glossary on page 23.

What is a lemur?

A lemur is a **mammal**.

Many mammals have hairy bodies and feed their babies milk.

There are many different types of lemurs.

The biggest lemur is the indri.

What do lemurs look like?

Lemurs have long arms and legs, and often have long tails.

Their strong hands and fingers help them to climb trees.

Lemurs have thick fur that can be brown, black, white, or red.

This lemur has **tufts** of fur around its neck.

Where do lemurs live?

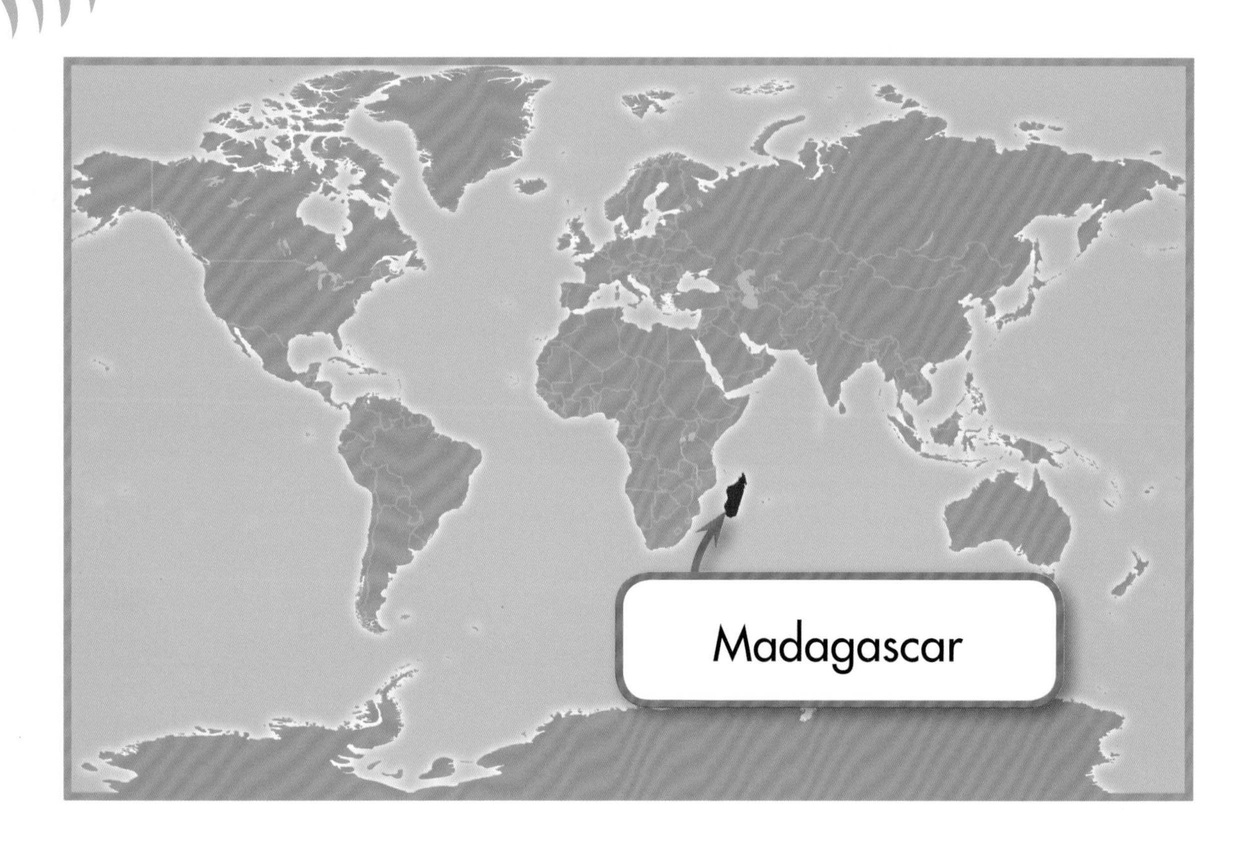

Lemurs live on the island of Madagascar in the Indian Ocean.

Wild lemurs are not found anywhere else on Earth.

The lemurs in this book live in **rainforests** on Madagascar.

It is warm and wet in the rainforest all the year round.

What do lemurs do in the day?

Many types of lemurs wake up when the sun rises.

Then they spend the morning moving through the trees and looking for food.

In the afternoon, some lemurs like to have a rest and sunbathe.

They sit on a branch and stretch their arms out wide.

What do lemurs eat?

Lemurs eat fruit, leaves, and seeds.

They also use their long tongues to reach deep inside flowers for food.

Some lemurs hang upside down from trees to feed.

They hang on to the branches with their feet.

Do lemurs live in groups?

Many lemurs live in groups of up to 20 animals.

A group is called a **troop**.

Living in a group helps to keep the lemurs safe.

Animals, such as **fossa**, find it easier to attack one lemur than a whole group.

What do lemurs sound like?

Lemurs make lots of different sounds.

They can wail, scream, snort, yap, and groan.

These sounds help the lemurs to keep in touch with each other.

They also warn other groups of lemurs to stay in their own space.

Where are baby lemurs born?

Some baby lemurs are born in nests in the treetops.

The female builds the nest out of twigs, leaves, and moss.

In the day, female lemurs carry their babies with them as they look for food.

Baby lemurs cling to their mother's belly or back.

What do lemurs do at night?

In the evening, the lemurs look for more food to eat.

Then they go to sleep on a branch, or in a hollow tree.

Some rainforest lemurs look for food at night.

Other lemurs move about from time to time during the day and night.

Lemur body map

Glossary

fossa meat-eating animal from Madagascar

mammal animal that feeds its babies milk. Most mammals have hair or fur.

rainforest thick forest with very tall trees and a lot of rain

troop group of lemurs

tuft bunch of something such as fur, that grows from the same place

Find out more

Books

Rainforest Animals (Focus on Habitats), Stephen Savage (Wayland, 2006)

Usborne Beginners: Rainforest, Lucy Beckett-Bowman (Usborne, 2008)

Websites

www.durrell.org/animals/mammals/redruffed-lemur

www.arkive.org/indri/indri-indri/

Index

babies 4, 18, 19
climbing 6
feeding 10, 12, 13, 20, 21
fossa 15
fur 4, 7
Madagascar 8, 9
mammals 4
movement 6, 10, 21
nests 18
noises 16, 17
resting 11, 20
troops 14, 15